A Steadfast Spirit

About the Cover
Bears embody strength, courage, tenacity, and nurturing.

The image, "Two Bears," on the cover of this book has been used with the permission of the estate of the revered artist, Harriet Johns. Harriet lived much of her life in the American Southwest and the San Francisco area. She was born on October 25th, 1923 and died on October 17th, 2014, at age 90. Bears appeared as a prominent theme in Harriet's work after her box-car home in Crestone, Colorado, was twice invaded by bears that left claw marks on the walls. These experiences rendered her afraid, but determined not to give in to dread. Instead, she connected with the bears' energy in a positive way by creating a spiritual offering to them. Through her art she was able to take control of the bears and her fear, and free her emotions from their powerful, terrifying presence.

A STEADFAST SPIRIT
THE ESSENCE OF CAREGIVING

Marian Leah Knapp

MARIAN LEAH KNAPP

Copyright © 2017 Marian Leah Knapp

All rights reserved. No part of this book may be used or reproduced by any means, graphic, electronic, or mechanical, including photocopying, recording, or taping, or by any information storage retrieval system without a reference to the source. Use this statement each time a citation is made: "From 'A Steadfast Spirit: The Essence of Caregiving' by Marian Leah Knapp, 2017, [Page], Loagy Bay Press, Chestnut Hill, MA."

Credits
Editor: Laurel J. Kayne
Proofreader: Pauline Chin
Resource List: Ariel Sherry
Graphic Design and Publication: Story Trust Publishing, LLC

Published by
Loagy Bay Press
Chestnut Hill, Massachusetts

Printed in the United States of America

ISBN: 978-0-9895470-1-7

To my Children & Grandchildren
Philip Eli, Vicki Ann, Hannah Rose, & Samuel John
Daniel Charles, Mari, & Lina Sakura

In Loving, Sad Memory
Sonia Joseph & Irwin Selikson

The Embodiments of a Steadfast Spirit
Barbara Semancik & Stephen Semancik

"…and renew a stedfast spirit within me."

Psalm 51:12

Contents

AT THE BEGINNING
25

IN THE MIDDLE: DAY-TO-DAY
35

AT THE ENDING
45

CONCLUSION
53

RESOURCES
59

Acknowledgments

I ACKNOWLEDGE THE PEOPLE who were involved in a multitude of spheres during my caregiving decades. First and foremost were the people I cared for in big and small ways. They profoundly influenced my learning; without them I would have been ignorant of the complexities and intensity of caregiving. I had primary responsibility for my mother and father, Anne and Louis Gilbert; my aunt, Lena Bobrow; my cousin, Frederick Weiner; my aunt, Celia Goldberg; and my aunt and uncle, Sylvia and Edward Goldberg. I was involved in a less encompassing, but still emotionally impactful way with Leon Knapp, Arthur Weiner, and Millie Woolf. My cousins Sonia Joseph and her husband Irwin Selikson's illnesses required a short-term, but excruciatingly concentrated immersion in the final days of their lives. I miss all of these treasured and unique people.

There were friends, relatives, and colleagues whom I relied on for wise advice, caring support, and simple kindness. They included Martha Kurz, Luanne Johnson, Annette Needle, Miriam Sack, Eileen Shaevel, Donna Soodalter-Toman, Jeanne Stolbach; all of my old-time "Jr. Debs"—Elaine Ades, Harriet Adelberg, Dorothy Carlin, Fredda Chauvette, Naomi Goodell, Reyna Katt, Soni Meyer, Rona Nachbar, and Wilma Walter; my nephew and niece, Joshua and Jennifer Gilbert;

my cousins Sonny Joseph and Irwin Selikson; and friends and colleagues Jayne Colino, Alice Bailey, and Azzie Young. My sister Paula Ruth Gilbert and my brother Arthur Gilbert contributed sincerely as part of the caregiving process. My spirit is grateful to Judith Gilbert and Bill Sutherland for their endless wisdom and compassion. Vivien Goldman was my stalwart empathizer; because she and I were going through the caregiving journey at the same time, we could console one another in ways that others couldn't.

My children and grandchildren were a constant mainstay of support, and at times, came to my rescue, especially when I had some health episodes for which I needed my own personal caregiving.

To those who helped with the production of this book—David O'Neil, Laurel Kayne, and Pauline Chin—I could never have done it without them. Special thanks to Ariel Sherry who doggedly investigated, read, and recommended the resource list at the end of the book.

Finally, I give my profound thanks to Reverend Howard Haywood, (Retired), Myrtle Baptist Church, Newton, MA, who inspired me to put this book together in the belief that it would help many people who struggle every day with the daunting responsibility of caregiving.

Introduction

ALL MEMBERS OF my family from the previous generation have died, and I had primary responsibility for many of them. This included my mother, my aunt Lena, and my aunt Sylvia. I was also involved, somewhat less intensely, with my dad because my mother was the principal caregiver. Sylvia took care of her husband Eddie after his stroke, except when I was watching over both of them when she was in rehab for months after having been hit by a car. Except for my mother, most of the others had no children to help them. My aunt Celia had two daughters who were far away and with whom she had a tense relationship. In her frequent hospitalizations or when she saw a doctor she put my name down as the contact person, and I responded. Whenever she was released from the hospital, I made sure she had food in the house. I was the one the hospital called when she was dying.

After my cousin Arthur died, I watched over his disabled brother, Freddie. He was my age and had been institutionalized most of his adult life. After deinstitutionalization, Freddie lived in a group home that was managed by the state. I held his health care proxy and, together with his niece, had to make significant health and end-of-life decisions on his behalf. There were other loved ones for whom I had a hand in caring, but I wasn't the main responsible person.

My caregiving started with my dad in 1987 and ended in 2013 with the death of my aunt Sylvia—a span of more than twenty-five years that included intimate caring for approximately eight relatives or friends. Truthfully, I have lost track of how many. With that extended, and at times all-consuming, experience, I am comfortable saying that I am a bit of an expert. I don't know every aspect of every condition that requires caretaking, but I have gone through a multiplicity of intense episodes, with the accompanying powerful emotions. It is in this that I am an expert.

I fit the description of a "caregiver [as] an unpaid individual (a spouse, partner, family member, friend, or neighbor) involved in assisting others with activities of daily living and/or medical tasks."[1] This statement sounds so simple. Its two lines have only seven key words or phrases: caregiver, unpaid, individual, assisting, activities, daily living, and medical tasks. To this list I add administration and after-death. But behind each word or phrase there is a massive footnote which, when opened, reveals numberless, complex, often daunting issues. Each word or phrase is worthy of an entire essay or even, perhaps, a book. I am not going to write a book on each subject, just this brief summary. I hope this conveys the overloaded life of caregiving.

Caregiver

According to AARP and National Alliance for Caregiving, in 2015, approximately 43.5 million people were providing care to someone who was ill, disabled, or aged.[2] The need for caregivers will grow among younger folks as our 65+ population continues to age. This demographic is expected to reach close to 73 million by 2030 and more

---

1 FCA Family Caregiver Alliance, https://caregiver.org/selected-caregiver-statistics Accessed 10/24/2014
2 Caregiving in the U.S., 2015, The National Alliance for Caregiving and the AARP, Public Policy Institute, www.aarp.org/content/dam/aarp/ppi/2015/caregiving-in-the-united-states-2015-report-revised.pdf Accessed 11/01/2016

than 20% of the total population. By 2040 it will be 80 million and by 2050 it will be 84 million.[3]

I, like most people, was never taught how to be a caregiver. I had to learn it on the job. With each new challenge, I had to figure out what the issues were, how to find help, how to make decisions, how to balance the rest of my life and, most importantly, how to stay sane. For everyone out there who is going through the same thing, I understand.

I faced a wide variety of challenges because of the unique personality, social situation, and medical circumstance of each "caree." I cared for people with heart disease, stroke, cancer, dementia, repeated aspirations and pneumonias, mental and physical disability, and lots of plain, old-age-related problems. People had trouble walking and used canes, walkers or wheelchairs. They were hard of hearing, on restricted diets, had vision problems, took lots of medications, were unsteady in the shower, and were often incontinent. There were medical, legal, and financial forms to fill out and submit, and clinical staff from many disciplines to talk to, learn from, and whose instructions I tried hard to follow. Four of my charges were in their 90s and were all declining at the same time.

There were always decisions to make, which ranged in importance from what type of walker was best, to whether to admit someone to a nursing home, to whether to sign a do-not-resuscitate order. I never questioned my responsibility to the people I cared about. It didn't matter if I liked doing it or not. The task was in front of me and I did it, often unprepared, and I did it unpaid. It was, for me, an unquestioned family obligation.

---

3 An Aging Nation: The Older Population in the United States, May 2010, U.S. Census Bureau, https://www.census.gov/prod/2014pubs/p25-1140.pdf Accessed 11/01/2016

Unpaid

Unpaid family caregivers will likely continue to be the largest source of long-term care services in the U.S. This will have major impact since the age 65+ population will "more than double between the years 2000 and 2030."[4] Both the Congressional Budget Office and AARP attempt to put a price tag on unpaid caregiving, with AARP's most recent estimate for the year 2013 coming in at a staggering $470 billion, up from an estimated $450 billion in 2009.[5] To put this in perspective, AARP compares the figure to Walmart's annual revenue, which in 2013 was just shy of $470 billion—putting unpaid caregiving on par with the world's number one ranked Fortune 500 company.

I was unpaid, but I never calculated the size of a hypothetical paycheck. For me there was no purpose in doing that. First, I cared for people because that was what I was supposed to do. I didn't want any compensation. Second, for much of my caregiving years I was an independent consultant with flexibility in my schedule, so I didn't have to dock hours from a job. Yet there were weeks when I couldn't go to meetings, work on client projects, or look for new opportunities. I probably lost thousands of dollars in billable income during those years, but I didn't tally it up. I was lucky to have enough to get by on. However, caregivers with regular work face a different and more complex set of issues as they shuffle or reduce work hours or take leaves of absence. The result is lost wages, health insurance, and other benefits. [6]

---

4 Coughlin, Joseph F. (2010). Estimating the Impact of Caregiving and Employment on Well-Being: Outcomes & Insights in Health Management, Vol. 2; Issue 1 - Updated: November 2012

5 Ianzito, Christina, AARP Blog, 07/16/2015, http://blog.aarp.org/2015/07/16/family-caregiving-worth-470-billion-a-year-aarp-finds/?intcmp=AE-BL-IL-BLOG Accessed 8/30/2015

6 Feinberg, Lynn, Susan C. Reinhard, Ari Houser, and Rita Choula - AARP Public Policy Institute, July 2011, Valuing the Invaluable: 2011 Update: The Economic Value of Family Caregiving. AARP Public Policy Institute. Updated: November 2012 http://www.aarp.org/relationships/caregiving/info-07-2011/valuing-the-invaluable.html Accessed 10/24/2014

Individual

Mostly I was on my own in caregiving, except for an occasional doctor and the kindness and compassion of good friends, my children, and a few family members, including my siblings who lived at a distance. Even with the help and guidance of others, I was the one who had to gather, sort, and decipher endless pieces of information. I had to decide which parts were critical, which ones were optional, and what could be discarded with or without guilt. Often people gave me good advice, but their words were bits of data to put in the large stewing pot for my consideration. Ultimately, I was the decision-maker. I remember many hours of sitting at home, walking in the woods or on the beach, and pondering the choices and decisions—alone. It was a solitary job.

The majority of people who take on the job of caregiving are like me—women. According to the National Alliance for Caregiving (NAC) and the AARP Public Policy Institute, 60% of caregivers are women, and 40% percent are men; 18% care for two or more people.[7]

Research studies report that the average age of a female caregiver is 48.[8] I was around 49 when I began my caregiving journey and 75 when it ended. When the average age is cited it only represents one point in time. The responsibility may last over a period of years as we age along with the people for whom we are caring. A 2011 Gallup study reported that over 50% of caregivers had that responsibility for three years or more.[9] Mine lasted for a whole lot longer. The estimates on years of

---

7 The National Alliance for Caregiving (NAC) and the AARP Public Policy Institute, Caregiving in the U.S. Washington, DC. June 2015 http://www.caregiving.org/wp-content/uploads/2015/05/2015_CaregivingintheUS_Executive-Summary-June-4_WEB.pdf P. 9 Accessed 10/17/2016

8 The National Alliance for Caregiving and AARP (2009), Caregiving in the U.S. National Alliance for Caregiving. Washington, DC. - Updated: November 2012 http://www.caregiving.org/data/ Caregiving_in_the_US_2009_full_report.pdf Accessed 10/24/2014

9 Gallup Healthways Wellbeing Survey, Most Caregivers Look After Elderly Parent; Invest a Lot of Time, July 2011- Updated: November 2012 http://www.healthways.com/solution/default.aspx?id=1125 Accessed 10/26/2014

caregiving don't say when the starting point is. We know what the end is—death—but when do we start counting? Also, what if, as in my case, someone is caring for three people at a time? Is that three years of caregiving or nine years' worth of expended energy?

Assisting: Activities, Daily Living, and Medical Tasks

The terms activities, daily living, and medical tasks are all sub-jobs in the larger category of "assisting." I can sort this assisting in different ways. All caregivers do some or all of these things.

There were activities intended to introduce some pleasure and to help the hours be less routine for both my caree and me. I arranged for family gatherings, having lunch or dinner, watching television, reading books, taking a drive, and just talking. When my mom was in the nursing home, I sat down with a small group of women and had a discussion, recorded their words, and called it a book of poetry, which I read back to them. I also put together a little song book of old favorites and brought it with me to the nursing home. Our group sang together for 10–15 minutes, enough time to keep within everyone's limited attention span.

I also did lots of daily living activities. I did grocery shopping, cooked meals, helped with dressing and undressing, bathing, eating, and driving to see friends or relatives. And, yes, I did toileting and cleaned people up after bowel accidents—not pleasant for them or me.

There were many medical tasks to take care of. I kept track of medications and picked up and administered prescriptions. I drove people to doctor and clinic appointments, and sat in on conversations so that I could hear and interpret when my caree couldn't. I applied cream to my mom's nasty eczema and comforted my aunt Lena when her dementia left her constantly pulling off her clothes. After a while, discussing illness and treatment options, visiting people in the hospital, and making end-of-life decisions became almost matter of fact.

Administrative Responsibilities

I faced another set of activities that often isn't mentioned. I call this administrative work. The activities involved financial chores, such as paying bills, balancing checkbooks, and dealing with Medicare, Medicaid, and hospital or nursing home administrators. There were also legal issues like helping to create wills and keeping them up to date, and making sure that appropriate health care proxies and powers of attorney were in place. Estate planning involved both financial and legal actions.

After-Death Tasks

After someone died there were finishing-up activities. I did this also, many times. There were funeral arrangements to be made if they had not been planned beforehand, and even if one had been arranged, I had to call the funeral parlor, meet with a representative, plan the details, write the obituary, order a death certificate, and notify people about the burial date. In my case, there were few people to tell since my relatives outlived almost everyone they knew intimately.

I cleaned out apartments and gave carloads of possessions to charitable organizations. Anything of value I distributed to people named in wills. The rest— personal items, medications, ointments, toothbrushes, and dented pots and pans—I threw out.

I was the executrix/personal representative of three estate settlements. Once all of the cleaning out was done, I met with attorneys and financial agents, closed bank accounts, created estate accounts, and then wrote any checks that were due to beneficiaries. This part lasted more than a year for each person. Even though the people had died, I was still taking care of them through the things they had left behind.

The Impact on Me

The impact on me was profound—sometimes extremely onerous and other times very rewarding. The hard part was the stress that resulted from stretched physical energy, consumption of time, conflicting obligations, and emotional fatigue. The physical aspect was the least of my problems. I remained in good health throughout the years of caregiving. I never had to lift a heavy person from a toilet or a bed. I learned early on that I had to watch my health if I was to continue to be a functioning caregiver. So I was very careful about what physical tasks I took on and when to find someone else to do them. Nobody—neither my caree nor I—had a physical accident when we were together.

Bad things did happen to my charges when I wasn't around, like falls, not eating, or incontinence. I tried to forgive myself for these incidences by telling myself that I couldn't be in three or four different places at once. I tried to keep the amount of guilt at a reasonable level, but it was always a nagging presence, and the level went up and down depending on the severity of the guilt-causing event. Missing a visit was not as bad as not being there to prevent a serious fall that ended up in a hospitalization.

The time consuming-nature of caregiving is linked to conflicting obligations. The challenge was always how best to use my time, either for the benefit of my caree or to shore up myself. Should I visit my loved one or earn some money to pay bills? Should I be on the phone for an hour to find a specialist or have lunch with an understanding friend? I worked hard to find the right balance, but it always involved anxious decision-making.

The most difficult times were when two or more of my folks were having serious problems simultaneously. It was not simply deciding whether to visit or not, but whose crisis was the biggest. Should I return home from a trip to oversee someone's emergency admission to the intensive care unit, or stay and take care of a relative who had just fallen and broken her knee cap? I came back for the person in intensive care.

The emotional stresses could be overwhelming. I think I got through it all partly because I accepted that there would always be another predicament to face and I had to be there to handle it. In a way, I was telling myself that I couldn't let all of the bad stuff get me down. I had to somehow float over it to be ready for the next event. I had to be steadfast in my determination and spirit. I found comfort among people who were going through the same thing. They understood in a way that others did not. Also, I knew that somewhere down the road it would be over. And it was, when my last relative died just a few years ago. However, I didn't realize the complete emotional impact on me until I was through it. Only when I had the freedom to look back did I wonder how I managed.

Caregiving has some cultural myths around it. Illusions around caregiving range from ideas like "if you tell people about the stresses of caregiving they will understand and be supportive," or "it's your job to make your loved one happy," or even, "it doesn't matter what you do, love will see you through."[10, 11] To all of these I say "definitely not necessarily true!"

As I reflect on those years, there were two extremely important impacts on me. First, caregiving made me realize who I was at the core of my being. I forced myself to watch my reactions to things and saw that deep down, for some unknown reasons, I was driven to take care of those who relied on me. This doesn't mean that I loved them all equally. I didn't. Some were easier to love than others. But it did not matter what their personalities were; I took care of them anyway.

---

10 CareGiving.Com. 2010, The 6 Myths of Caregiving http://www.caregiving.com/2010/01/the-6-myths-of-caregiving/ Accessed 10/26/2014

11 The Practical Caregiver Guides. Myths of Caregiving. http://www.practicalcaregiverguides.com/caregiver-myths Accessed 10/26/2014

Something within my innermost essence made me do it. It felt as if I had no choice. I suppose I could have fought the impulse to provide care, but I didn't. It felt like destiny. I didn't know what was inside of me until I was confronted with the realities of the sick and aging people I worried about. Because of caregiving, it is much easier now for me to know what is most important to pay attention to in my life, what I must hold on to, what has lesser significance, and what I can let go. Some of that wisdom comes from my own aging experience. But mainly, I think, it comes from being a caregiver. I am profoundly different from the way I was 30 years ago, and I find that immensely satisfying. Knowing that I have grown and changed gives me a sense of clarity and peace.

The second impact from caregiving was the realization that I had to make the most of my own life going forward. Many relations on both sides of my family lived to be well over 90, and most of them didn't start to decline until they were around their 90th year. When the bulk of my caregiving began in the late 1990s, I was in my 60s and realized that if I were to live that long, I had to do something with the 30 years I may have left so I could look back at some meaningful achievements. That is when I decided to go back to school and to bring what I learned into my family and community to help in whatever way I could—particularly around supporting people as they get older. That is exactly what I am doing now in my late 70s.

Caregiving was a life-changing, perception-altering, and personality-developing experience. I would not have learned about the person I really am without it. I would never have gone back to school. I would never have found a life focus. And I would never be contributing in the way I am now. I am deeply, deeply grateful.

This book has three sections representing the unstoppable caregiving process that has a vague Beginning, a daunting, lengthy Middle, and an unambiguous End. The essays are written from my own journeys through this natural life course. I try to explain what I went through and the influence that this had on me. I hope my words resonate with your own experience, and that you find some solace knowing that there is someone out there who understands. You and I are not alone.

AT THE BEGINNING

We Are Not Prepared

AN ACQUAINTANCE RECENTLY commented that she had heard that caregiving was a bit like being a first-time parent with no experience in raising a child. To some extent this is correct. If someone hasn't nurtured a baby through childhood and beyond it is hard to know what to do. I remember the angst I felt trying to do the right thing for my kids when they were young, particularly with my first born. Even with a good deal of support, I only learned what really worked through experience.

Just as I was never adequately prepared to be a parent, I was not prepared to be a caregiver. Because I had no older people in my growing-up years, I never saw the realities of getting old until my parents began to visibly age. It was only after having taken care of people in decline that I knew what I was up against.

Although there are a few similarities between raising children and taking care of elders, such as the constant attention required, there are immense differences. The first is about the nature of the relationships. Kids are impressionable, with limited knowledge of the world around them. In contrast, older people have decades of experience and accumulated learning. They are likely to have strong opinions and routines that must be respected. If we make an unpopular decision for a child, we could end up with disgruntlement. If we try to make a disliked decision for an older adult, we can end up denigrating who she or he is as an independent, thinking being.

The relationship between a parent and child is usually clear. There are precedents for defining the association. This is not necessarily true for the relationship between an adult and an elder. With each change in status for the older person, the relationship may be redefined, resulting in more authority for the caregiver and a decrease in power and loss of control for the elder. This is an extremely difficult situation for both people and can be fraught with the complex emotions of distrust, guilt, uncertainty, and fear of the unfamiliar.

The second main difference is that with raising children there are systems in place to rely on and from which we can expect some reasonable response. These include education, medicine, sports, and social networks. We learn about what is available simply by being part of a well-established, child-oriented community in which information is shared among parents in routine, everyday conversations. Just by being parents we belong to peer groups with common concerns. Although systems and resources for elders and their caregivers may exist, there is no natural community for passing on knowledge about caregiving. We are individuals on our own.

The third, and perhaps most significant, is that early on in raising a child we begin to learn what is out there to tap into. Our knowledge gathering about childhood has an extended history, beginning prior to birth and continuing into their adulthood. With elders, our quest for information often begins with a crisis, or at the least, in an urgent situation. Unlike the process for youth, the path for growing older often has no long-term planning connected to it. If a problem arises, we suddenly have to figure out how to deal with it.

Truthfully, it may not even be that we don't know how to find help. A bigger issue may be that we don't want to acknowledge age-related decline. The symptoms of decline might be occurring right before our eyes in our daily lives, but it is easier to look away than to accept it. This denial prevents us from planning and impedes efforts to become informed about available resources. In reality, there are many services, but we avoid investigating them because it is too painful to recognize that our loved ones (or we) are getting older. The result is a profound lack of preparedness.

I am not being critical of this behavior. I acted this way in my own caregiving experience. I denied that my mother, aunts, uncle, and cousin were declining. Not facing the truth, however, left all of us confused and conflicted. I am not advocating that we obsess about aging, but I do advocate for thinking pragmatically about the overall decisions we might have to make for others and for ourselves—ideally before a critical situation develops. By doing this early, we are far better prepared for the moment when we need to make a thoughtful change that will set a sensible path for the future.

Anticipating a Team: For them and for us

Most of my caregiving experiences have been with people who were old and who were living through conditions that develop over the aging process. I dealt with dementia, heart disease, cancer, and strokes.

If I had known better at the start of my caregiving journey, I would have tried to figure out what we may need along the way. The "we," of course, was first my "carees" and then me. At the beginning my main focus was, appropriately, the people I was taking care of. They were the ones who eventually would require services from doctors, dentists, attorneys, audiologists, financial advisors, social workers, pharmacists, housing and transportation experts, home care providers, nursing homes, and hospitals. The list of needs varied by person and also changed over time. At first, not everyone required extensive home care, for example, but with greater and greater decline, the need for more hours of assistance increased.

My mother, aunts, uncle, and cousin each required something different, and I had to search for the right kind of support. My mother wanted to relocate and we arranged a move for her to be closer to me. My aunt Lena wanted to stay in her long-term apartment forever, despite her obvious decline. My cousin Freddie was already in a group home and well taken care of. My aunt Sylvia strongly resisted leaving her seriously unsafe house. Yet in these different situations there were decisions to be made. The quests for solutions were endless and exhausting, and I stumbled through the entire way. Sometimes I found the appropriate resource, sometimes I didn't. There were times when I gave up looking, especially when the problem was not likely to have a solution worth implementing before inevitable death.

Because of my lack of previous caregiving experience, I didn't recognize until well into the process that, in addition to caree requirements, I needed some sympathetic, reliable backing of my own. This was especially evident when I had to make decisions about who among my carees needed me the most and then balance their situation with what I had to do to take care of myself. There were times when the effort to find a new audiologist, for example, seemed far less significant compared to my own critical need for a few hours of quiet rest. Sorting through and balancing these dilemmas resulted in even more guilt and stress.

Reflecting now, I see that I would have benefited from having two teams. One for clinical and social service management for the benefit of the people I cared for, and the second one for me and my well-being. The caree's team initially would have included the caregiver (me), my caree, a primary care physician who ideally would have expertise in geriatrics, plus a facilitator or care manager who could have helped guide the process. The four of us would have met together, identified current situations and diagnoses, and discussed the impacts on health and quality of life now and into the future. We would have laid out a strategy to pave as smooth a road as possible for moving forward together. We would have set a regular check-in schedule to address shifting issues. The goal would have been to avoid last-minute, crisis-mode decision-making. Discussions would center on the areas where difficulties frequently develop during aging. This includes establishing a relationship with a reliable health care system; assuring safe and accessible housing; finding transportation options if driving is no longer possible; obtaining in-home medical and personal assistance—either short- or longer-term; creating ways to stay socially engaged to avoid isolation; and making certain that financial, insurance, and legal documents are in order—including Social Security, Medicaid, Medicare, and end-of-life decisions.

In initial meetings we would have identified potential complicating factors along with the related special medical or social issues. At this point it would not have been possible to know the exact impending circumstances, but at least we would have established a core relationship to build upon. The facilitator would have been there over the long-term as circumstances shifted, offering advice and recommending resources.

Identifying the members of a team wouldn't have been a prediction of doom and distress, but rather an information-gathering exercise. An investigation into resources would have been quite matter-of-fact and would have involved simply keeping a list of names and numbers to call when the time came. It wouldn't have been worth trying to anticipate all of the possibilities that might emerge, but some general contact information would have been helpful, such as links to local senior services agencies, AARP, or for specific needs, the Alzheimer's Association, American Diabetes Association, or the American Cancer Society—all of which offer suggestions for caregivers. (These and other organizations and some books are included in the Resources section of this book.)

All of this team-building for a caree sounds great, but it is a fantasy that I have created after the fact. The reality is that the barriers to creating a support system like this are daunting, especially (and ironically) for a process that is predictable and omnipresent. First, depending on where we live, there may be a lack of clinicians with geriatric expertise, so we may need to rely on primary care providers who may or may not have skills and knowledge about aging. Second, primary providers of care and services often don't have the time for sit-down planning meetings with patients, caregivers, and other members of an interdisciplinary team. Finally, even if this were possible, you and I as caregivers would still have to be the everyday organizer, driver, and implementer of this management system, even with the help of a facilitator or care manager. Creating a care system while someone is still living in the community would be extremely difficult because we wouldn't know potential needs until they happened, and therefore we wouldn't know, in advance, what help to seek. Also, services are often in silos that don't always communicate easily with each other.

In my caregiving, I did ultimately connect with organized systems over the years, but they were in long-term care facilities or hospitals where protocols existed for bringing me together with representatives from multiple disciplines. We had meetings, discussed issues and options, and identified resources as needed. But there was a huge gap of organized support before a caree moved into a long-term facility from which they would never leave.

If I were to do it over again I would plan for what happens while someone I was caring for was living at home. I would go to the National Association of Area Agencies on Aging web site, find my local Area Agency on Aging (AAA), and locate a geriatric primary care physician and other services for my caree and for me. I would contact my local

Council on Aging or Senior Center and ask for a list of resources. I would start the information gathering before uncontrollable, precipitous decline set in. I would try to think about the most likely scenarios. I would act sooner rather than later.

For the second team—my team—I would try to understand what I might need for myself over time and begin building resources to support me. In the beginning, this would be pretty hard to do since I didn't appreciate what I required until after the caregiving had been going on for a while. Still, I could have taken a first step and contacted the Family Caregiving Alliance and learn what was available in my area. Again, I would contact my local Area Agency on Aging and senior services agencies, which are likely to have caregiver support groups. Above all, I would find one or more friends whom I could count on to listen and to understand. I would make sure we had coffee or lunch every few weeks. I would ask them if it was OK to pour out my frustrations—and offer to return the favor.

In order for any of this planning to happen, I would have had to take a huge mental and emotional leap and acknowledge that a person I loved was going to weaken and die, and that I needed help dealing with it. I think that some of the biggest barriers to taking this leap are denial and fear. First, none of us wants to accept the fact that those we love (and ourselves) are going to get old, possibly sick, decline, and die. Over and over, I hear stories about a good death. "He just went to bed one night and didn't wake up. That's how I want to die." Certainly this easy way of dying happens occasionally, but it is far more likely that there will be a period of deterioration and then a relatively short time— maybe days, weeks, or months—in the slide towards death.

There are probably many explanations for why we deny the aging and dying process. One may be the popular fantasy that we will remain young forever. Staying young is far nicer to think about than getting old. Another common reason and one that helps perpetuate the forever-young syndrome, is fear of being sick, in pain, losing our dignity, and dying. We may be afraid of taking away a person's independence or becoming dependent ourselves.

It wasn't until I was caring for my last elder that I was able to confront the denial and fear, and take some actions that were difficult but necessary. By the time my aunt Sylvia was declining, I knew what was coming. Having become wiser and more confident from my earlier caregiving experiences I took charge. I changed her health care providers because I thought her current ones weren't paying enough attention. I convinced her to sell her tear-down house and move into a condo, and then into a nursing home. Although she was very angry at me, I knew she was going to be in good hands in her final months. It was a great loss for her to give up her independence, and I understood that. But, I realized that my goal had to be finding ways to help her retain self-esteem rather than keep her in an unsafe place. Ultimately, though, she told me she was relieved. The decision for her to relocate gave me peace of mind. I no longer worried about her falling down the rickety stairs to her laundry room in her basement. I stopped getting calls at 2:00 a.m. to ask me if she should call 911. And I didn't have to rush out in the middle of the night and hold her hand until she calmed down. She was safe and I could sleep.

IN THE MIDDLE: DAY-TO-DAY

Emotions of Caregiving

I LOVED THE PEOPLE I cared for—mostly. I resented them too sometimes, but not often. It was only when I was exhausted to the point of despair that I got cross at them. Not anger really, but irritation and frustration. I was tired and weary so much, because my whole life was frequently dictated by their needs. My annoyance stemmed primarily from their not having prepared adequately for the end of their lives, or at least that is what I felt back then. Now that it is over and I can think with a greater degree of reason, I realize that they really tried and did the best they could to make it easy for themselves and for me. Mostly, they got rid of a lot of unnecessary stuff prior to major decline and left only what was important to them in their ongoing lives. This included the pieces that held the memories of both good and even unhappy events, such as family photographs, old letters, a hand-me-down ceramic bowl, and a World War II veteran's army medals.

Although they tried to prepare each in their own way, what they couldn't do was know exactly what would happen to them at the end and plan how to deal with it. How could they know that they would have a stroke, or a heart attack, or undiagnosed cancer? There is no way that they could have been prepared for being unable to walk, having memory problems, or experiencing unremitting fatigue from unknown causes.

I don't really know what my carees felt as they went through this progression towards death. But they seemed to have been experiencing despair and intense frustration either because they wanted to live or they wanted to die. I could only watch, try to respond to what appeared to be going on, and face tough decisions. My aunt Lena wouldn't sign a do-not-resuscitate order, and no one had thought to make custodial and end-of-life plans for my disabled cousin, Freddie. In both of these cases, I was left with uncertainty about what to do, anguish in the decision-making process, and disquiet when I made choices that may have been contrary to a person's wishes. Occasionally I felt guilt, but not that often. I worked hard to accept the fact that I was doing what I could in each situation. I made conscious efforts to push guilt into the background. For me it was an unnecessary and futile emotion to hold on to.

In my caregiving years, my reactions weren't always logical, but I found that logic didn't always hold sway in situations where emotions were raw, immediate, and overwhelming. The intensity of those feelings varied depending on who I was taking care of. Perhaps because of my deep love for my mom and Aunt Lena, watching over them elicited the most feeling. They were both so much a part of my childhood and adult life. They were always there, always caring, and always with me. Interestingly, my emotions were not as intense for my aunt Sylvia. She had a personality that excluded people, making it hard to really love her. Because of her standoffish nature, it was easier for me to be objective and confront her about the issues that were swirling around her, and ultimately simpler to make decisions about what should happen in the last days of her decline. Even though she said she hated me at times because I made decisions she didn't like, she was ultimately able to tell me that I helped change her negative perspective on people. She had a tendency to not trust anyone and I tried to show her that it was better to trust and be hurt once in a while, because not trusting made it impossible to develop true, intimate relationships.

I think my caregiving emotions were so intense partly because I was unprepared for the arduous nature of the work. Those feelings are deeply embedded in me. Even now, if someone shares their ongoing caregiving experience I tend to project my own reactions and feel worn out even before I offer compassion.

Once death came to the people I took care of, I believe that the emotions of caregiving impacted my reactions to mourning. Certainly I was sorrowful at the losses, but mostly I felt released from the seemingly never ending load that was sitting heavily on my shoulders and deeply in my spirit for so, so long. I am different now. I miss the people I took care of. I miss the ability to share common history and recollections with them. I feel the lack of having the connections to these wonderful, good, and kind people. But I have folded these feelings into all of the other parts of me and created a new me—someone who understands the emotions of caregiving but who now wants to move on.

It's Impossible to Explain

Some of the most difficult and frustrating times I had being a caregiver came when I tried to explain what it was like to someone who had never faced this task. I would talk about challenging episodes with personality issues, health care system negotiations, arguments about insurances claims, and most of all just the inexorable, iterative patterns of watching over someone for a long, long time. Daily routines in these extended periods involved making sure someone was eating properly, was safe where she was living, and bringing her to appointments. Then there was all of the waiting—endless waiting—for a call back from a doctor, for prescriptions to be filled, or for insurance to come through.

I could spout words of explanation to numerous people who would ask how I was doing and each would react differently. Some would immediately understand because they too had been responsible for someone. What a huge relief it was when that happened. Knowing that there was another person out there with caregiving experience made me feel that I was not alone. Most of the time, support came from my kids, friends, or even casual acquaintances. Occasionally there was a clinician who gave good advice and pointed me in a concrete direction, but these instances seemed dribbles of assurance in an overwhelmingly complex, vast, and confused universe.

Other people would look at me as I started to talk about taking care of someone and within seconds their eyes would glaze over, and I knew that they didn't get it. They didn't understand, or couldn't understand, because they had never done the job themselves. Sometimes they would make suggestions that made no sense. "Maybe your mom could benefit by learning how to use a computer?" was one suggestion. At the time, my mom was already physically diminished by falls and frequently disoriented from small strokes. She couldn't comprehend what a computer was let alone how to use one. As innocent as this proposal was, it led to additional effort for me because I wanted to respect the person who made the suggestion. I had to talk to a computer instructor (who thought it was an untenable idea) and go through (again) why this made no sense when I already knew it in the first place. This added time and ate up some of the precious minutes I had in each day. It jammed an irritating wedge into an already tightly compacted aching mass.

Even worse for me was when people suggested things that I had already tried and didn't wait for me to explain why their plan wouldn't work or, in some cases, could be harmful. I knew from experience, for example, that it was best if my mom sat in the front seat of a car. The seat in the front was slightly higher than the one in the back, making it easier for her to get in and out. She was a tiny person, and every inch of horizontal or vertical space made a difference in how easy or difficult it was for her to negotiate her world. Very occasionally, others with good intentions transported her in the back of the car and tried to convince me that it was a better way. I could see how she struggled more to get out, but they didn't. I grudgingly stayed silent when this kind of thing happened because I didn't have the emotional strength to argue. These examples seem minor, even silly, but it was not one or two infrequent events that had an impact. It was the layering of incidents one upon another, creating what felt like a simmering mass of frustration. I can't really say what the impact was on my mom because I wasn't the one who had to get in the car or be confused by a computer. I was the observer, the worrier, and the responsible one.

When I talk to people about what it is like to be a caregiver I can see immediately from their faces who has held this job. Their complexions pale dramatically. Their bodies seem to shrink as if they are still carrying the overwhelming weight, and their voices become subdued as if they don't have a lot of energy to even talk about it. When this happens, I only need to nod my head and say, "I know, I know. I've been a caregiver many times." They are relieved because they don't have to try to explain. Because I really know, I am able to convey my profound and sympathetic understanding of what they are going through. If you find yourself with the role of caring for someone, gently put aside those who can't listen, can't understand, and will never be able to support you in the way that you deserve. Find people who have gone through the same experience. You will never have to expend precious energy trying to describe the reality. They already grasp its enormity.

The Very, Very Bottom Line

I am often asked if I have any advice for people who are taking care of aging loved-ones or are getting older themselves. There are no universal answers to questions about caregiving, so how I respond will depend largely on the particular issue and the physical and mental status of the caree. Often, advice can simply involve providing information about a particular resource, like home delivery of books from the library, or how to find options when someone no longer wants to drive. This is the easy part.

It becomes extremely difficult for both caregivers and carees when the time comes to face a decision that could be life-altering and contrary to someone's wishes. There are two major areas where the safety of an individual and a potential negative impact on others are at stake. These are driving and housing.

Fortunately, driving concerns arose for me in only one caree situation. My mother was wise enough to give up her car voluntarily when she was involved in two minor accidents in a parking lot. She was very clear. "I shouldn't be driving anymore," she said. Lena had given up her car years before because she lived in Boston and could walk or take public transportation anywhere she wanted to go. It was a different scenario for Sylvia. She lived in the suburbs, had a car, and was determined to keep driving because that represented her powerful independence and her ability to take care of herself. But, because of her weakening health status, I could see that she shouldn't be driving. She was a hazard to herself and others. It wasn't that she was oblivious to her problem because she expressed concern that she could harm someone if she faltered at the wheel. Yet she couldn't, on her own, take that step to stop driving.

In actuality it was more the idea of driving than the fact of it. She had dramatically curtailed her driving a few years before she died, but was hoping to get back to it once she felt better. She had her car routinely serviced in expectation of that day. I was able to use her health as a delaying tactic by saying that we had to see what the doctor said.

The doctor suggested a "driver improvement" course but also pushed for waiting to see what happened. This was a huge relief for me. I never had to take away Sylvia's keys, but I would have if the doctor hadn't backed me up.

After driving, the other major scenario that may require a bottom-line decision is whether someone is safe where they are living. Again, my mom was the ideal caree. She made the decision to move into an Independent Living facility[12] near me. My aunt Lena always insisted on going back to her apartment after her many hospitalizations or stays in rehab facilities. She felt passionately that the only way for her to get better was to take a bath in her own tub. During her last stay in rehab, she wanted to leave and bathe at home, but the staff and I wouldn't let her go. She was obviously too frail—weighing about 80 pounds—and disoriented. She hated the idea that someone was making the decision for her, but despite her determination, she didn't have the wherewithal to make it happen.

Ultimately, I had to make the decision for Sylvia to leave the house where she and my uncle Eddie had lived since after World War II. The final episode that convinced me was when her chimney was backing up and emitting noxious odors inside that she did not smell. She vehemently fought the idea, but the same bottom-line issue was true. She wasn't safe, and the incessant need to monitor her was having a serious negative impact on my own well-being.

I started out as a caregiver wanting and assuming that I would be able to respect and carry out someone's wishes until death. After all, as a society, we value an individual's right to live their lives in the way they choose. Certainly, I would want to apply this principle to myself. Yet, I discovered that I couldn't live up to this ideal. I knew that it wasn't just about taking care of an older person. It was also about tak-

---

12   Independent Living facilities offer meals, social activities, cleaning and personal services, but no medical care.

ing care of me. So there were two of us that needed caregiving, and I ended up being the one making the decisions for both.

I have been reproached by some who believe that an individual's right overrides every other consideration. And, yes, there are those who will forfeit their own well-being in order to serve someone else. I applaud them. But I couldn't do it. I never abandoned anyone, but I didn't sacrifice my own life for wishes that were impossible to achieve without serious health or emotional consequences for me. Before I made life-altering decisions for other people, I spent unsettled days and nights filled with anxiety and guilt. However, once I created two bottom-line questions to ground me—"was my caree safe?" and "could I manage the situation without putting myself at risk?"—I was able to put other considerations and circumstances in practical perspective, and their importance gradually faded, becoming almost background noise.

I stopped feeling guilty. Rather, with these two questions to ground me, I felt strong and certain that I was doing the right thing, and the decisions I made still seem right after a number of years. The sad reality was that my carees could no longer make reasonable decisions. I had to take over and choose for them. I didn't like doing this, but I had to—for their safety and my survival.

AT THE ENDING

End-of-Life Decisions

Over the course of ten years I made end-of-life decisions for three unique individuals: my mother, my aunt Lena, and my cousin Fred. I was the health care proxy for all of them. In spite of good care, thoughtful interventions, and supportive environments, each was on a path towards dying. Frailty was the only thing they had in common. It's easiest to start with my mom because hers was the simplest decision. My siblings and I knew her well enough to anticipate her wishes with certainty. After having lived independently until her early 90s, she entered a nursing facility because she needed 24-hour care. She signed a do-not-resuscitate order.

But most of her time in the nursing home she just sat—waiting. Over three years she became less engaged and more inert. Then she stopped eating. I figured she didn't like the food, so I made special things. But when I presented the fork she clenched her mouth shut. One day I offered egg salad (her favorite) and she slapped my hand away. Stunned at her aggression, I finally realized it was her way of telling me she was ready to die and I needed to let her go. It was her decision—not mine. So I stopped trying, and together we waited quietly until she died peacefully a few weeks later.

Lena was different. The same age as my mother, she was determined to live. When she was 93 I admitted her to a rehab facility after she became dangerously thin and was constantly trying to undress. She refused to sign a DNR order. The medical staff suggested that I sign. My two adult sons said I should, but her sister-in-law Celia said, "Lena would want you to do everything to keep her alive." What was I supposed to do? Here was a woman who wanted to live, and I had to decide if I could honor her wish. But Celia called back with a gift of trust. "Lena probably would not want to live in that condition," she said, "and besides, it is your decision, and I will support whatever you think is right." The next morning, as I was leaving to sign the DNR, the doctor called to say that Lena had died during the night. She spared me the act of signing but not the agony of the decision.

My cousin Freddie, just a few months older than I, began having seizures when he was a toddler. Epilepsy was poorly understood in the 1940s, and treatment was largely an uncharted field. No matter what therapies were tried, he continued to seize, fall, and suffer head injuries, which in combination ultimately limited his capacity to understand complex issues. In his late teens, when his parents could no longer take care of him, he was placed in a state hospital where he lived for about 40 years until the Department of Mental Retardation's de-institutionalization policy moved him into a group home. When Freddie's parents died, his brother Arthur took over responsibility. When Arthur was dying from cancer I told him I would watch over Freddie.

After a few years, Freddie began to aspirate food, resulting in multiple hospitalizations and debilitating pneumonias. Freddie never had a legal guardian, but his care team suggested that I become his health care proxy. The law requires that, without prompting, an individual must name someone to make decisions in the event that they are not able. The problem was that Fred couldn't understand what that meant. He kept saying he would make decisions for himself. Finally, with several witnesses present, he named me as his decision-maker. I faced only one medical choice—whether or not to give Freddie a feeding tube. I wrestled with what his parents or brother would have done and consulted with his niece. Ultimately, I decided not to order a feeding tube, knowing that it wouldn't prevent ongoing problems. Hospice was brought in, and after several pneumonias, Freddie died at home among friends.

Three people—one who wanted to die, one who wanted to live, and one without the capacity to make reasoned choices. Making decisions for someone close to the end of life can be daunting or relatively simple. It depends on whether thoughtful planning and communication occurred well before the approach of death. I learned, through hard experience, the necessity of naming a proxy and providing enough information so that she or he can decide with as little anxiety and guilt as possible. I experienced the ordeal of making a decision contrary to someone's wishes. Most importantly, I discovered the power of trust—a gift that only we can give to those who will carry out our own end-of-life decisions.

The End of Caregiving

I sat down today and figured out that I was a caregiver of older loved ones for varying amounts of time and intensity for much of the past 30 years. It started with my dad who died in 1987 at age 83. He had a major stroke about six months earlier and was totally incapacitated—no speech, swallowing, walking—nothing. His mind was still working because he tried to spell out words to express his needs and feelings. "How are you feeling, Dad?" I would ask. "D….E….A….D" he responded. It was agonizing to watch. My mom, who was 79 at the time, was still healthy and able to bear most of the responsibility for watching over him in the nursing home. She didn't want to drive across town every day, so she hired a driver, Bernie, who took her back and forth, and who provided consistent friendship and kindness.

My father's situation gave me my first exposure to what it meant to be a caregiver, but I really didn't understand the complete reality because my mother took on the major burden. I would go to Rhode Island where they lived as much as I could, but mostly I was a loving, sympathetic observer and supporter rather than an active participant in caregiving.

After my dad died, my mom continued with her life with friends and activities, along with my somewhat peripheral involvement, for about 10 years. In 1997, at age 89, my mother decided to sell her condo and car, and move to be closer to me. She had begun to have some health problems and I was going back and forth to R.I. more and more frequently. She wanted to make things easier on me, so she relocated.

In retrospect, I think this was the beginning of when caregiving became a major part of how I spent my time and, perhaps more significantly, emotional energy. During the next 6 years, in addition to my mother, I watched over my aunt Lena, aunt Celia, my cousin Fred, my uncle Eddie, and finally, Eddie's widow, my aunt Sylvia, who died in December 2013 at age 94. A few of these people had a family member who carried a bit of the load, but the remainder had no one else to care for them except me. At one point, my mother, Lena, and Eddie were each in different hospitals at the same time. I went from one hospital to another visiting them, talking to doctors, nurses and administrators, and making plans for discharge. That was about all I could do. Much of the rest of my life was on hold.

Then, within a relatively short number of years, my mom, Lena, Celia, Fred, and Eddie declined and died. Each circumstance was unique, involving lesser or greater hands-on caregiving, but all requiring decisions on health, living situations, dying, death, and burial. In several instances I executed wills and settled estates. As of 2008, only

Sylvia was alive. She was pretty independent at age 90. She and I tried to see each other frequently, often going out to lunch at ethnic restaurants. Then she began to decline and, again, I was involved in all of the issues I had previously managed with everyone else, until she also died. She was the last in the long list of family elders.

Sylvia's death, for me, meant the end of caregiving. There is no one else of that older generation that I will be responsible for. Unless something untoward happens with someone of my generation, I won't be taking care of any other old person. I have to say that I am extremely relieved. I have gotten through the worry, anxiety, confusion, exhaustion, and stress of caregiving, and I am coming out the other end of what feels a bit like a long murky tunnel. I am glad to be at this end.

This summer I am taking advantage of a place I have had on Cape Cod for 40 years but where I never spent any time. I had to rent it for all those years in order to keep it. This past fall when I got the rental forms from my real estate agents, I looked at them and asked myself, "wait a minute, if not now, then when?" I decided to spend the summer here.

The end of caregiving has allowed me to do these things—sit peacefully and watch the glaring orange sun set over the deck, ponder the long, dark pine-tree shadows that flicker all over me and my space, and have a nice glass of wine. I am not worrying about someone's health emergency; I'm thinking fondly about my kids and grandkids. I do profoundly miss the people who are gone from my life, but on the other hand, I am just here being me and feeling free. It is wonderful. There were times over the years that I couldn't imagine what life after caregiving would be like. Now with all of the responsibility gone from my everyday existence, I know there is a future because I am living it.

CONCLUSION

Supporting a Steadfast Spirit

My caregiving days are mostly over. There may be a few people who will need my help in the future, but I will never again take on the full load. Partly this is because someone younger will likely have the total responsibility, but also because I really don't want to do it anymore. It isn't even that I feel I have fulfilled all obligations. It is more that I am older, a little more tired, and doubtful that I could once again summon the steadfast spirit that being a caregiver requires.

Upon reflection, I realize that I have been fundamentally changed by the caregiving experience. On the surface I am the same person, continuing with my regular life, but internally I am different. Each time I see an older person with a cane or walker, accompanied by a younger person, I feel the emotions of both the senior and the caregiver. I know their dilemmas, and I feel sadly resolute knowing what they will go through—fearful denial and gradual adjustment, disorienting confusion and ultimate resolution, anxious frustration and welcomed gratitude, and acceptance of the end of life.

Caregiving has changed my perceptions about life. It has influenced decisions about how I want to exist into the future. Caregiving taught me how to distinguish what is important and what is insignificant, and it has compelled me to try to think consciously about my next steps.

Acknowledging the end of my caregiving days is positive and freeing, but at the same time poignant. I feel I did a good job taking care of loved ones. I know that even the curmudgeony ones appreciated it. However, caregiving has been so much a part of my life that not doing it anymore feels as if a core piece of me is floating away. Of course I will still care about the people who I am close with, offer help when I can, but someone else will be in charge. This is a relief but also a loss.

To mitigate that sense of loss I can keep myself in the action by continuing to plan for my own aging and by helping others, including my children, to have an easier time being steadfast as they take care of me. There are many good books on caregiving and I have listed some of them in the Resources section. I don't need to repeat the good advice within these resources. I offer a few ideas to think about. Use them as you will.

For Caregivers:

It is hard to give advice to caregivers because everyone's situation is different. But there are a few things that are worth contemplating.

- Don't deny that someone you love is declining.
- Talk to your caree early on, if possible, to find out what her or his wishes are.
- Talk together about what you think your role may be.
- Do the least threatening thing by gathering information about resources for a future time.
- To whatever extent possible, respect your caree's wishes.
- Identify, acknowledge, and respect your own needs and wishes.
- Trust your judgment, but find a friend to validate your view.

- Don't let anyone second guess you and cause you to expend limited energy on unconstructive suggestions.
- Don't feel guilty if you can't be in multiple places at a time or know everything there is to know.
- Know that you are doing the best you can.

For Yourself and Your Future Caregivers:

I am struck by the fact that although I have learned a lot from my experience, I am still a bit reluctant to apply that learning to myself. There are two major reasons why I must push myself to acknowledge and act on my own aging. The first reason is me—to keep myself in control for as long as I can. The second reason is to make caregiving easier for those who will take care of me—in my case, my children.

The first thing I did was to downsize and move into a building with one-floor living and people to take care of shoveling snow and regular maintenance. This relocation required that I get rid of more than half of my accumulated stuff, but I still have too many things I don't really need. I must continue to work on that.

The second thing was that I got organized. I gathered and sorted important papers and information and created a "Document List," which is a simple inventory of relevant documents and where they are located. This list includes the obvious things such as my name, telephone, and social security number, but also the names of key providers and contacts such as my doctor, lawyer, and insurance policies. It catalogues all of my legal documents such as birth certificate, last will and testament, durable powers of attorney, and medical directive, and where all of these documents can be found. It shows bank information and passwords, in case my designated legal representatives have to pay bills on my behalf. I have met with my kids to show them everything so they know where to go and what to do if I can't act on my own. (I have included a draft "Document List Form" below.)

I'm not sure what my next steps will be except to keep being mentally and physically active, and not deny that I continue to get older. Caregiving has prompted me to recognize the importance of creating a path for those who will ultimately be my caregivers. I know that one day I am likely to be in a position and condition similar to those I took care of. It may be just a few years from now, or perhaps twenty. But it will come. What I need to do now is to plan well enough so that my children will have a caregiving journey that is more informed and less burdened than mine has been. I know that I can't make it stress-free for them, but I want to use my knowledge to help them get through it as peacefully as possible.

RESOURCES

Books

Here is a short list of books that may be helpful and supportive during the caregiving journey.

Bayley, John. 1999. *Elegy for Iris.* St. Martin's Press, NY

Read this book to gain insights into the complexity and poignancy of caring for someone with Alzheimer's disease.

Bayley, a literary critic writes about his wife, the renowned author Iris Murdoch, and her gradual, devastating decline. This book was made into a film in 2001 and starred Judi Dench and Jim Broadbent.

Chast, Roz. 2014. *Can't We Talk about Something More Pleasant?* Bloomsbury USA, New York

Reading this book helps you visualize yourself as a caregiver and provides a little reality check when things seem overwhelming.

This wonderful, cartoon-format book conveys the dilemmas, decisions, and intense emotions that the author experienced in caring for her parents. It is full of humor, frustration, poignancy, and, most of all, honesty.

Edmunson, Janet. 2006. *Finding Meaning with Charles: Caregiving with love through a degenerative disease.* JME Insights, Portland, ME

This book will help people who are caring for someone with a disease with no cure.

The author cared for her husband for six years from 1995 in the early stages of Parkinson's disease to his death in 2001. The book records the journey and is dotted with "Caregiving Affirmations" that identify meaningful lessons from each step in the difficult process.

Gawande, Atul. 2014. *Being Mortal.* Metropolitan Books, Henry Holt and Company, LLC, New York

> *This book is good to read at the beginning of your journey caring for someone with a long-term illness.*

> Over many years, the author cared for his father who had a spinal cord tumor. The author, a physician, profoundly explores how the experience challenged his own assumptions and helped him confront the inadequacies of his professional training in end-of-life care.

Gross, Jane. 2012. *A Bittersweet Season.* Vintage Books, Random House, New York

> *Use this book to validate your own frustrations and fulfillments as a caregiver, and to gain insight into how, and why systems do or do not work.*

> The author draws on her experience caring for her mother and explores the inadequacies of systems that care for the elderly. She identifies caregiver learning opportunities about common age-related issues and conditions.

Loverde, Joy. 2009. *The Complete Eldercare Planner: Where to Start, Which Questions to Ask, and How to Find Help.* Random House Press, New York

> *You'll find tangible steps that guide you through a number of caregiving situations.*

> The size of the book may seem daunting but it is broken up into small, readable sections. Use the table of contents to direct you to specific topics. The wide range of topics helps you prepare and deal with many situations. It offers worksheets and lists of additional resources.

Lunden, Joan and Amy Newmark. 2012. *Chicken Soup for the Soul: Family Caregivers: 101 Stories of Love, Sacrifice, and Bonding.* Chicken Soup for the Soul Publishers, LLC.

> *At any point in time and for any issue you can pick a topic, and quickly read someone's thoughts and suggestions.*

> The authors want to prepare people for caregiving. They offer four simple pieces of advice: "…asking more questions when I could still get answers (p. 8)"; call a family meeting (p. 9); "…interview and record our parents…,(p. 10); and "…keep the love connection going" (p. 11). Individual stories confirm and underscore these messages.

Mace, Nancy L. 2006. *The 36-Hour Day: A Family Guide to Caring for People with Alzheimer Disease, Other Dementias, and Memory Loss in Later Life.* 4th Edition. Johns Hopkins Press Health Books, Baltimore

> *Turn to this book to gain understanding of specific dementia-related circumstances such as behavioral, medical, housing, driving, and daily care issues.*

> It includes some general advice for caregivers and explains the roles of professionals. Sections are short and labeled so readers don't have to read the whole book to get some helpful advice.

Meyer, Maria, with Paula Derr, RN. 2014. *The Comfort of Home: A Complete Guide for Caregivers.* 4th Edition. Care Trust Publications, Portland, OR

> *This book is primarily for people who are caring for someone at home.*

> It offers advice for the beginning stages of caregiving and dealing with day-to-day issues. It is written in a simple format and provides concrete suggestions on the nitty-gritty of caregiving such as pre-

paring the home, financial considerations, and nutrition. This is a good book to have as a reference to pick up when needed.

Morris, Virginia. 2014. *How to Care for Aging Parents: A One-Stop Resource for All Your Medical, Financial, Housing, and Emotional Issues.* Workman Publishing Company, New York

Go to this book when you need advice on specific issues.

The book is dense and would be overwhelming to read as a whole. However, it covers topics such as how to talk to your parent about finances or how to help your aging loved one with daily living. Organized into short sections outlined in the table of contents, this book provides guidance on how to approach situations, quotes from other caregivers, and helpful boxes with quick facts and checklists to save you time.

Murphey, Cecil. 2011. Illustrations by Michael Sparks. *When Someone You Love No Longer Remembers.* Harvest House Publishers, Eugene, OR

Go to this book when you only have a few minutes to read, but enough time to ponder the messages.

There are twenty-four brief and meaningful essays in this tiny volume with exquisite watercolor paintings. Although this book has a Christian orientation with many Old and New Testament quotes, everyone can find comfort in the thoughts conveyed.

Samples, Pat. 1999. *Daily Comforts for Caregivers.* Fairview Press, Minneapolis

Use this book to identify short readings for comfort whatever your spiritual identity may be.

This book consists of one-page meditations for each day of the year on the multiple, intense emotions of caregiving. An alphabetical listing helps the reader to find a topic that is important to her.

Span, Paula. 2009. *When the Time Comes: Families with Aging Parents Share Their Struggles and Solutions.* Springboard Press, Hachette Book Group, New York

You will find good stories, suggestions, and questions to ask about living situation decisions: home care, moving in, assisted living, nursing homes, and hospice.

The author, a journalist, considers her book "as a support group in print (P. 21)." Using stories from family caregivers, she investigates the complexity of caregiving and the wealth of solutions created by those who chose to assume this weighty responsibility.

Web-Sites

There is a great deal of information available nationally, by state, and within local communities. Here are some entry points on caregiving and specific areas of concern that will lead to additional resources.

The Conversation Project: http://theconversationproject.org/

The Conversation Project is dedicated to helping people talk about their wishes for end-of-life care. They offer a "starter kit" to help begin the conversation about end of life.

Family Caregiver Alliance: https://caregiver.org/about-fca

This site can help individuals to find support services for caregivers in their location.

Making Care Easier: https://www.makingcareeasier.com/about

> This free online tool helps "families find, store and share personalized information, actionable how-to lists, products and professional service providers." It makes it easier for families to coordinate care.

National Association of Area Agencies on Aging: http://www.n4a.org/

> n4a offers The Eldercare Locator which produces brochures on topics for older adults, caregivers, and professionals. Brochures can be viewed online or ordered.

National Council on Aging: http://www.ncoa.org/

> "The National Council on Aging (NCOA) is a respected national leader and trusted partner to help people aged 60+ meet the challenges of aging." Look at their *5 Resources for Family Caregivers*.

Specific Conditions and Diseases:

Many specific conditions and diseases have web sites that offer information and resources. For other resources, search the internet for the name of the condition or disease.

Alzheimer's Disease and Dementia: Alzheimer's Association. http://www.alz.org/

Cancer: American Cancer Society. http://www.cancer.org/treatment/caregivers/

Diabetes: American Diabetes Association. http://www.diabetes.org/living-with-diabetes/recently-diagnosed/8-tips-for-caregivers.html

Parkinson's Disease: National Parkinson Foundation. http://www.parkinson.org/about-us.aspxoc

Local Resources

Senior Centers and Councils on Aging: Cities and towns have resources for seniors through either Senior Centers or Councils on Aging. Check your local government web site or contact city or town hall for information.

Document List Template

Document List for (Name): _____

Address: _____

Telephone: _____

Telephone: _____

Telephone: _____

E-mail: _____

Personal Information: _____

Critical Document Storage Location: _____

Other Document Storage Location: _____

Other Document Storage Location: _____

Name at Birth: _____

DOB: _____

Hospital: _____

City/State: _____

Birth Certificate Location: _____

Social Security #: _____

Driver's License #: _____

Parents' Names: _____

Parents' Address: _____

Parents' Telephone: _____

Key Providers/Contacts (General)

Health Provider/Insurance: _____

Health Insurance—Supplemental: _____

Primary Care MD: _____

Dentist: _____

Periodontist: _____
Hearing/Audiology: _____
Eye Care: _____
Specialist: _____
Specialist: _____

Non-Health Care Providers

Attorney: _____
Accountant: _____
Financial Advisor: _____
Broker: _____
Insurance Agent: _____
Real Estate Agent: _____

Other Key Contacts

Cleaning Service: _____
Computer Advisor: _____
Web Developer: _____
Building Manager: _____
Contractor: _____
Plumber: _____
Electrician: _____
Trash: _____
Grounds/Landscape: _____
Painter: _____
Handyman: _____

Location of Personal/Legal Documents

List of Codes and Passwords: _____

Birth Certificate: _____

Last Will & Testament: _____

Durable Power of Attorney: _____

HIPAA Privacy Authorization and
Release of Protected Health Information: _____

Health Care Proxy: _____

Medical Directive: _____

Trust Documents: _____

Passport: _____

Social Security Card: _____

Medicare Card: _____

Other: _____

Other: _____

Location of Funeral and Burial Arrangements

Funeral Arrangements: _____

Burial Arrangements: _____

Income

Social Security: _____

Pension: _____

IRA—Minimum Required Distribution: _____

Investment Income: _____

Other Income: _____

Financial/Investment Accounts:

*Uses these accounts for writing checks before selling investments or property.

*Bank: _____
*Bank: _____
Bank: _____
Bank: _____
Bank: _____
Investment Account: _____
Investment Account: _____
Investment Account: _____

Loans

Mortgage: Original documents: _____
Mortgage: Lender : _____
Loan: _____
Loan: _____
Loan: _____
Credit/Debit Cards: _____
Credit Card: _____
Credit Card: _____
Debit Card: _____
Debit Card: _____
Store Credit/Debit Card: _____

Property/Automobile

Residence: Deed: _____
Residence: Deed: _____
Automobile: Title: _____
Other: _____

Insurance

Homeowners Insurance: _____
Homeowners Insurance: _____
Automobile Insurance: _____
Long-term Care Insurance: _____
Road Service: _____

Taxes

Real Estate Taxes: _____
Real Estate Taxes: _____
Personal Property: _____
Excise Tax : _____

Health, Dental, Long-Term Care Insurance

Health Insurance—Primary Insurance: _____
Health Insurance—Medicare: _____
Health Insurance— Supplemental: _____
Long-Term Care Insurance: _____

Assets (may need separate page)

Property Value: _____

Property Value: _____

Electronic Equipment: _____

Artwork: _____

Jewelry: _____

Furniture: _____

_____

_____

Furnishings: _____

_____

_____

_____

Additional Items

_____
_____
_____
_____
_____
_____
_____
_____
_____
_____
_____
_____

Made in the USA
Middletown, DE
29 April 2017